STARTERS
DINOSAURS

Written by
Nick Pierce

Illustrated by
Fabrizio Di Baldo

SCRIBBLERS
a SALARIYA *imprint*

This edition published MMXIX by Scribblers,
an imprint of The Salariya Book Company Ltd
25 Marlborough Place,
Brighton BN1 1UB
www.salariya.com

SALARIYA
SCRIBO BOOK HOUSE SCRIBBLERS

© The Salariya Book Company Ltd MMXIX

PB ISBN-13: 978-1-912537-23-5

3 5 7 9 8 6 4 2

A CIP catalogue record for this book is available
from the British Library.
Printed and bound in China.
Reprinted in MMXIX.

Printed on paper from sustainable sources.

Visit
www.salariya.com
for our online catalogue and
free fun stuff.

Consultant:
John Cooper studied Geology at university and
began a career in museums, specialising in the
study of dinosaur fossils at Leicester Museum
and the Carnegie Museum in Pittsburgh, USA,
before moving to Brighton to become Keeper
of Natural Sciences at the Booth Museum
of Natural History. He is the founder and
chairman of the Brighton & Hove Geological
Society and has written many children's books
on geological themes. He retired in 2015 but
remains the Emeritus Keeper of Natural
Science at the Booth Museum.

Contents

Introduction

The dinosaur age (the Mesozoic era) began 225 million years ago. At that time Earth was covered in thick forests and dusty plains. The climate was much hotter than it is now. There were no mammals, flowering plants or birds.

The dinosaurs that roamed among the shrubs and trees in search of food were reptiles. They were relatives of the snakes and crocodiles that live on Earth today. Dinosaurs would survive on our planet for the next 160 million years.

On each spread you will have to look for different objects in the main picture.

5

Dinosaur museums

Can you find...?

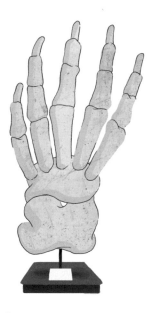

Our first introduction to the world of dinosaurs often comes from visiting museums that contain fossils and models of different species. Seeing these life-sized replicas of animals that once walked the Earth helps us to imagine the lives of dinosaurs.

▲Dinosaur models

Copies of dinosaur bones are made and joined together to make life-sized models of different species.

▲Bones in museums

Sometimes complete skeletons of dinosaurs are made from exact copies of bones to help keep the originals safe.

◄How many species?

More than 700 different types of dinosaur have been discovered.

◄ Dinosaur bone
Can you find this bone in the picture?

▲ Plant
Can you find this plant in the picture?

▲ Display case
Dinosaur fossils are often presented in glass-topped display cases for protection.

▲ Eoraptor
This is a model of an Eoraptor. This meat-eating dinosaur lived in South America. It was about 1 metre (3.2 feet) long.

► Palaeontologist
Museums often employ dinosaur experts, called palaeontologists, to share their knowledge of dinosaur fossils with visitors.

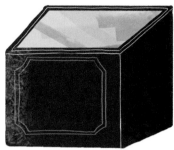

Dinosaur diets

Can you find...?

◀Diplodocus
One of the longest dinosaurs, Diplodocus, was about 27 m (88 ft) long. Its long neck helped it to reach the leaves of tall trees and plants.

▲Tyrannosaurus rex
Tyrannosaurus rex was one of the biggest meat-eaters that ever walked on earth. It hunted other dinosaurs, using its powerful back legs to chase and attack its prey.

◀Triceratops
Plant-eaters like Triceratops were toothless. They had beaks to crunch through tough tree trunks.

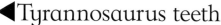

◀ Tyrannosaurus teeth

Tyrannosaurus rex had strong jaws and sharp teeth. The largest tooth ever found is 30 cm (12 in) long.

▲ Stegosaurus

Stegosaurus was a herbivorous (plant-eating) dinosaur that lived in the Jurassic period in North America. It had a brain the size of a walnut.

▲ Gastroliths

Scientists think that dinosaurs, like Stegosaurus, probably swallowed stones to help grind food to a paste in their stomachs. These stones are called gastroliths.

Like most animals living today, dinosaurs were either meat-eaters or plant-eaters. Plant-eating animals are called herbivores. Some of the biggest dinosaurs were herbivores. Species like Plateosaurus were slow-moving and had to eat a lot of plants every day just to survive. Meat-eating animals are called carnivores. Huge meat-eating dinosaurs hunted other dinosaurs, even plant-eaters that were much bigger than they were. They would usually attack and kill the weakest dinosaurs.

▶ Stegosaurus plates

The crest of jagged plates on the back of a Stegosaurus probably helped it to adjust its body temperature.

Dinosaur eggs

Many fossilised dinosaur eggs have been found. Some dinosaurs laid eggs just like birds and reptiles do today - they simply scooped out a hole in the ground for their nests. The first fossilised dinosaur eggs were found in Mongolia, China, in 1923. They are about the size of a large potato and are probably the eggs of a Protoceratops.

Can you find...?

▲Maiasaura

These dinosaurs grouped their nests close together. They laid batches of around 12 eggs that were long and rounded in shape.

▲Protoceratops

Protoceratops laid its eggs in a hollow in the ground.

▲Oviraptor

The name Oviraptor means 'egg-thief'. It was once believed that they stole and ate the eggs of other dinosaurs. This has been proved wrong.

Giant dinosaurs

Some dinosaurs were the biggest land-living animals ever to have lived on Earth. Large size was a useful protection against other meat-eating dinosaurs. Being so big also meant that they kept warm and active for longer. The largest known dinosaur was Argentinosaurus, thought to be about 40 m (130 ft) long. It lived in South America about 95 million years ago. Brachiosaurus had a neck that was nearly 9m (30 ft) long.

Can you find...?

▲Trees
How many trees can you count in this picture?

▲Compsognathus
This species of carnivorous dinosaur was small. It was about the size of a turkey.

▼Brachiosaurus
This huge herbivorous dinosaur was probably about 13 m (42 ft) tall.

Flying reptiles

Can you find...?

▲ Insect
Can you find this insect?

▲ Pterodactylus diet
Young Pterodactylus had few teeth and fed on insects; adults had around 90 needle-like teeth, and fed on fish.

◄ Pteranodon
Adult male Pteranodons had a wingspan of about 6 m (20 ft). This pterosaur had a gigantic crested head and jaws.

◀Rhamphorhynchus

This small pterosaur had 34 razor-sharp teeth for catching and eating fish. Its long tail trailed behind it like the tail of a kite.

▲Rock

Can you find this rock?

Dinosaurs could not fly, but a group of reptiles called pterosaurs could fly. They had wings made of skin. The word 'pterosaur' means 'winged lizard'. They appeared around 228 million years ago, and were the first animals known to fly, apart from insects.

▲Pterodactylus

Pterodactylus means 'winged finger'. It had a fourth finger at the end of each wing. Its leathery wings stretched from its fourth fingertip to its ankles.

Meteor!

▲ **Meteor**
Its impact crater was about 180 kilometres (110 miles) wide.

▲ **Plants**
Without warmth or light, all plants stopped growing and died.

Dinosaurs, along with more than half of the world's plants and animals, died out about 65 million years ago. Scientists believe that this happened because an enormous chunk of rock from outer space - a meteor or an asteroid - smashed into the Earth. Clouds of dust from the impact blocked all heat and light from the sun, plunging the planet into a cold darkness that may have lasted many months or even years.

▲ **Dinosaurs**
The plant-eating dinosaurs starved first. Meat-eating dinosaurs then died when their food source ran out too.

17

Finding fossils

Palaeontologists find the fossilised bones of dinosaurs buried in rocks. They dig up the rocks and bones together, wrap them up carefully and take them to museum workshops. There they finally remove the bones completely and begin to piece the dinosaur together. This giant jigsaw puzzle can take years to complete.

Can you find...?

▲Digging
The first step is to dig up the dinosaur bones. The rock surrounding the skeleton must be carefully chipped away.

▲Cleaning
This worker is brushing tiny fragments from a bone.

▲Transporting
Fossils are very fragile and must be treated with care. Bones are wrapped in tissue paper or plaster bandages.

Timeline

252 million years ago
This is the Triassic period.
Small dinosaurs have
begun to evolve.

200 million years ago
The start of the Jurassic
period. The first flying
reptiles appear.

231 million years ago
The earliest dinosaur
fossils date from this
time, known as the
late Triassic period.

125 million years ago

This is the late Cretaceous period. Tyrannosaurus rex and Triceratops appear and birds had evolved from the dinosaurs.

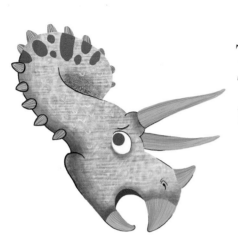

150 million years ago

This is the late Jurassic period. Large dinosaur species such as Diplodocus emerge, and so do the earliest mammals.

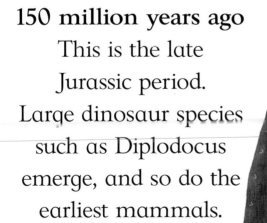

65 million years ago

The dinosaurs become extinct, probably because of the after-effects of a meteor hitting the Earth.

Quiz

1. What is the name for dinosaur bones found in the ground?

2. When did dinosaurs become extinct?

3. Which flying reptile had a crested head and huge wings?

4. Which huge herbivorous dinosaur lived between 152 and 145 million years ago?

5. Which dinosaurs grouped their nests close together?

6. What is the name of the stones that some dinosaurs swallowed to help digest their food?

7. Can you name one of the largest meat-eating dinosaurs ever?

8. What is the name for an expert who studies dinosaur fossils?

9. Roughly how many different species of dinosaur have been discovered?

10. What dinosaur species was about the size of a turkey?

Answers:

1. Fossils
2. 65 million years ago
3. Pteranodon
4. Brachiosaurus
5. Maiasaura
6. Gastroliths
7. Tyrannosaurus rex
8. Palaeontologist
9. 700
10. Compsognathus

Glossary

Carnivore A meat-eating animal.

Cretaceous The period from 146 to 65 million years ago. Dinosaurs disappeared at the end of this period.

Digest The process of food being broken down in a creature's stomach and absorbed into the body.

Fossil The remains of a dead animal or plant, naturally preserved in the ground.

Gastrolith A stone swallowed by an animal to grind up its food.

Herbivorous A diet of plants.

Jurassic The period from 208 to 146 million years ago.

Mammal A warm-blooded animal.

Mesozoic era The age of dinosaurs, from 245 to 65 million years ago.

Meteor A rocky or metallic object from outer space that sometimes crashes into a planet such as Earth.

Palaeontologist A scientist who studies fossils to learn about extinct animals and plants.

Triassic The period from 252 to 201 million years ago.

Index